W9-BZH-483

WITHDRAWN
No longer the property of the
Boston Public Library.
Sale of this material benefits the Library

Top Fuel

Drag Racing

by Martin Hintz and Kate Hintz

Reading Consultant:
Kendall L. Pyle, Ed.D.
National Hot Rod Association

CAPSTONE PRESS
MANKATO, MINNESOTA

C A P S T O N E   P R E S S
818 North Willow Street • Mankato, MN 56001

Copyright © 1996 Capstone Press. All rights reserved. No part of this book may be reproduced without written permission from the publisher.

Printed in the United States of America.

Library of Congress Cataloging-in-Publication Data
Hintz, Martin.
    Top fuel drag racing/by Martin and Kate Hintz
    p. cm. -- (Drag racing)
    Includes bibliographical references and index.
    Summary: Describes top fuel dragsters and their sport; includes a
history.
    ISBN 1-56065-389-2
    1. Drag racing--Juvenile literature. [1. Drag racing.] I. Hintz, Kate. II.
Title. III. Series: Drag racing (Mankato, Minn.)
    GV1029.3.H56 1996
    796.7'2--dc20

96-22345
CIP
AC

FIELDS CORNER
OCT 1997

Photo credits
Archive, 8, 14. FPG/Jeffrey Sylvester, 26. Don Gillespie, cover, 12, 17, 20, 28, 42. Martin Hintz, 22, 30. Steve Mohlenkamp, 4, 6, 11, 18, 24, 34. NHRA, 38, 41. Unicorn/Scott Liles, 33.

FC BR
J
GV1029.3
.H56
1996

Table of Contents

Words in **boldface** type in the text are defined
in the Glossary in the back of this book.

Chapter 1
Top Fuel Drag Racing

Dragsters are cars made for quarter-mile (400 meters) racing. Top fuel dragsters are the fastest dragsters in the world. A top fuel dragster does not look anything like a street car. It is long and skinny.

Drag races are tests of **acceleration**. The cars start from a complete stop. Top fuel dragsters reach speeds over 300 miles (480 kilometers) per hour. Top fuel drivers can finish a race in under five seconds.

Top fuel dragsters are the fastest dragsters in the world.

Top fuel drivers must pass tests to earn their racing licenses.

Drivers

Drivers earn their racing licenses only after many hours of driving. They take tests to move through the different racing **classes**. Top-fuel drivers have to prove that they are skilled long before they actually race.

Drag racing is a fast, exciting sport. Many people think it is fun to watch top drivers test their skills. Drivers try to match their best times whenever they race. Race fans like the speed and the roar of the cars.

Pit Crews

Mechanics keep the cars in top racing shape. Mechanics are often called wrenches. Each car's team of mechanics is called a **pit** crew. Pit crews can replace or repair any part quickly.

A semitrailer hauls the cars, the pit crews, and their tools from track to track. The semitrailers are like rolling garages. They even carry several back-up engines.

Some fans get a pit pass. It allows them to hang out in the pit area. They can watch mechanics get a dragster ready to race. They can ask questions.

Chapter 2
History

Drag racing started in Southern California in the 1930s. Drivers raced on city streets. They raced from stoplight to stoplight. Whoever made it to the end of the block first was the winner.

These early drag races were not very safe. There were many accidents.

Racers moved outside of town. They looked for straight, flat land. They raced on country roads, on abandoned airport runways, and in the desert.

Early drag races were not as safe as drag races today.

Eventually, local racing clubs were organized. They established rules and safety standards.

The First Drag Race

The first organized drag race was held in 1950 in Santa Ana, California. The National Hot Rod Association (NHRA) was formed the next year. A man named Wally Parks started the NHRA. He is known as the father of modern drag racing.

The NHRA set the official length of a drag-racetrack at a quarter-mile (400 meters). A car could go all out in that distance without damaging its engine. Drivers could go very fast and still come to a safe stop.

The first national championship was held in 1954 in Great Bend, Kansas. Today, the NHRA **sanctions** races across the United States and Canada. Drivers know that sanctioned events will be safe and well run.

Faster and Faster

Over the years, top fuelers have gotten faster and faster. Fans were amazed when these dragsters reached 200 miles (160 kilometers) per

Nearly every year, top fuelers go a little faster than they did the year before.

hour. Eventually, even the 300-mile (480-kilometer) per-hour mark was passed.

In 1994, Kenny Bernstein set a record of 312 miles (499 kilometers) per hour. In 1995, Bernstein shattered his own record. He reached 314 (502 kilometers) miles per hour at a race in Pomona, California.

Fans enjoy watching the top fuelers set new records. Nobody knows how high the speed record can go. Nearly every year, the dragsters go a little faster than the year before.

Chapter 3
The Cars

Top fuel dragsters are V-shaped. Top fuelers look like skinny insects. One top fuel dragster is called the Praying Mantis.

Like many other sports, top fuel drag racing has entered the computer age. Today's top fuel dragsters are designed with the help of computers. Mechanics use computers to keep them running well, too. At drag strips, starts and timing are controlled by computers.

Top fuelers can be up to 300 inches (762 centimeters) long. The driver sits in the widest section of the dragster. The frame of a top fueler is made of strong steel tubes.

Top fuelers are V-shaped. They look like skinny insects.

Engines

The first top fuelers had engines in front of the driver. Eventually, the engines were moved to the rear. This gave the dragsters better **traction**.

It is also safer to have the engine behind the driver. If there is a fire, the flames go toward the rear. They do not go in the face of the driver.

Engines often burn out in one season or less. This happens because they are worked so hard during a race. Racing teams have several spare

Early top fuelers had engines in front of the drivers.

engines. If an engine blows up during a race, mechanics can replace it.

Power

Mechanics do many things to make engines more powerful. They use a supercharger. This forces fuel into the engine at a higher pressure and temperature.

They use fuel injectors and **headers** to boost power, too. Fuel injectors force fuel into an engine's cylinders. Headers allow the exhaust to exit the engine quickly.

Top fuel dragsters burn a fuel called nitromethane. Nitromethane is commonly called nitro. Sometimes racers mix in other chemicals, too. These are called exciters. They make the fuel burn faster. A top fueler uses three to four gallons (about 15 liters) of fuel for each race.

Wheels

A top fueler's front wheels are small, narrow, and light. The wire spokes slice easily through the air. This cuts down on wind resistance.

A top fueler's rear tires are called slicks. They have no tread so more rubber touches the track. They are about three feet (about one meter) wide.

Only five pounds (about two kilograms) of air pressure is put in each tire. The heat and force of the spinning make the tires expand. A tire with too much air in it could explode.

A wing-shaped piece of metal is mounted on the rear of top fuel dragsters. It is called a

Top fuel dragster tires are called slicks.

spoiler. When air rushes over it, it pushes down on the rear of the dragster. This gives the cars better traction.

Chapter 4
Safety

Both cars and drivers must meet high safety standards. Each car is inspected by track officials. A team can enter the pits only when its dragster is approved.

Even the audience has to think about safety. Dragsters are very loud. Most fans wear earplugs so they do not damage their hearing. Drivers, mechanics, track workers, and safety crews wear earplugs, too.

Driver Safety

Each driver wears a helmet, a fire-resistant suit, a mask, goggles, and gloves. Each driver

Top fuel drivers must wear a full set of safety gear.

is buckled into a harness. In case of an accident, a latch releases the harness. This allows the driver to escape easily. Harnesses are inspected and replaced often.

Protection is built into the design of a top fuel dragster. A roll bar surrounds the driver. In a crash, this padded steel bar prevents the driver from being crushed.

The area at the end of the track is called the shutdown strip. There is where the cars slow down. A safety team is always on duty there. If a car's brakes fail, it runs into a sand trap at the edge of the track. The sand stops the car quickly.

Fuel and Oil

Fuel can leak from a car's tank if there is a crash. The fuel can burn or explode. Safety crews must get to the driver immediately.

The safety crew has fire extinguishers, axes, and crowbars. They have giant chain saws that

If there is an accident, safety crews are prepared to put out fires.

Safety crews make sure that races, racers, and fans are safe and secure.

can cut through metal. Sometimes they need a powerful tool called the jaws of life. The jaws of life can pry open a smashed car.

If oil or fuel is spilled on the track, a car could spin out of control. Safety crews clean up any spills. They use a piece of equipment called a track sweeper. A track sweeper is like a street sweeper.

The People in the Crew

Safety crews wear fire-resistant suits, heavy gloves, goggles, and helmets. Some safety-crew members are professional fire fighters who work part-time at a track. Others are full-time professionals.

The NHRA safety team is known as the safety safari. They travel to events across North America. They make sure races, racers, and fans are safe and secure.

Ambulances are ready at all races. Medical teams are ready at both ends of the track. If a driver is injured, the ambulance rushes him or her to the hospital.

Serious injuries are rare at a drag race. But anything can happen. Safety crews are there just in case.

Chapter 5
The Drag Race

On race day, drivers gather their cars in rows near the starting line. The rows are called staging lanes. The cars are called forward when it is their turn to race. Two cars compete in each **heat**. Cars race in classes. This makes the races fair.

The Burnout Box

Workers pour water and chemicals under the rear tires of cars about to race. The drivers rev their engines. Their left feet are on the brakes. Their right feet are pushing the accelerator pedals.

Drivers clear debris from their tires in the burnout box.

The cars stand still, shaking while the tires spin. The drivers are burning oil and other **debris** off the rear tires to get better traction.

This process is done in an area that used to be called the bleach box. When drag racing first started, bleach was poured under the tires. But bleach often overheated and caused fires. Bleach is not allowed at most tracks today. People today call it a burnout box or water box instead of a bleach box.

Christmas Tree

A pole called the Christmas tree sits between the two racing lanes. It is 20 feet (six meters) ahead of the starting line. There are two rows of red, yellow, and green lights on the tree. There is a row for each car.

The light at the top of the tree is yellow. When it blinks on, the drivers move from the burnout box toward the starting line. A second yellow light flashes when the dragsters reach the line.

The Christmas tree tells drivers when to get ready and when to go.

Then three more yellow lights flash. These lights warn the drivers to get ready. Sometimes a red light flashes. It means one of the drivers started too soon. That driver is **disqualified**.

When the light turns green, both cars race ahead. The noise is **deafening**. There is an electronic timing board at the far end of the track. It shows the winning time.

By the time two cars have finished their run, two others are in the burnout box. They are ready for the next heat.

Every professional drag strip has a timing tower.

The Timing Tower

The timing tower is a tall building near the starting line. From the tower, the race director controls the event. The director makes sure everything runs smoothly.

Timers also work in the tower. Their computers record the cars' speeds. From the tower, the announcer tells the crowd what is happening.

The burnout box is near the tower. When dragsters clean their tires, the vibrations shake the tower. Everyone has to shout to be heard

above the noise. Smoke rises in the air, making it hard to see.

Other Workers

There are many workers at a drag strip. Some of them line up the dragsters in the staging lanes. They direct drivers to the starting line. They keep an eye on things from the ground.

The track manager and the staff advertise the races. They sell tickets and keep the track and grandstands clean. They help reporters write articles about the races.

Some workers inspect cars. Some pump fuel. Some make sure there are enough hot dogs on hand for hungry fans.

Two Types of Racing

There are two types of drag racing. One is called heads-up racing. In this type, both cars leave the starting line at the same time.

The other type of racing is called bracket racing. In this type of racing, racers receive an

Some workers make sure the track is clear of debris.

average time in **preliminary trials**. This is called a dial-in time.

The dial-in time is written on the windshield with white shoe polish. Drivers try to match their dial-in times during the race. A dial-in time is also called an elapsed time or an e.t.

One driver's time might be slower than another's. The slower driver is given a head start. The faster driver is given a **handicap**. The handicap is the difference between the drivers' times.

Say one racer's dial-in time is 10.00 seconds. Say the other racer has a dial-in time of 9.50 seconds. This means that the first racer will get the green light .50 seconds before the other racer. This makes the race fair.

Top bracket drivers are consistent. They almost always match their average times.

After the Race

The cars are towed to the pits after the race. The driver is given the official race time on a slip of paper.

Top bracket drivers almost always match their average times.

Race teams compare the time to the driver's other races. They might need to adjust the engine. Repairs might be needed. Then mechanics start working right away to make the car run better.

Chapter 6

Track Speedsters

Top fuel drivers are the royalty of the drag racing community. They work on their own cars so they know how to get the best performance out of their dragsters. Professional drivers make a career of racing. When they win, they collect prize money.

Sponsors

Top fuel cars are very expensive. Teams need money for race cars, parts, insurance, transportation, food, lodging, and salaries. Sponsors help the teams pay the high costs of racing.

Sponsors put their names on the dragsters.

Shirley Muldowney's Top Fuel Dragster

Track Official

Spoiler

Roll Cage

Racing Slicks

Sponsors are oil companies, automobile equipment manufacturers, or other businesses. They put their logos on the cars. Often, a driver's uniform is covered with sponsor logos.

The best drivers have the most sponsors. Sometimes the drivers are paid by the sponsors. Cash prizes might be split between a driver and a sponsor. Drivers have to win races to keep their sponsors.

Supporting a winning racer is good advertising for a business. Sponsors want to be

Sponsors put their logos on the dragsters.

thought of as the choice of the champions.
Then they can sell more of their products to
both racers and racing fans.

Life on the Road

Even a top driver's life is not all glory.
Sometimes teams have to drive all night to get
to the next track. They grow tired of eating fast
food and staying in motels.

The team's semitrailer can break down on
the road. A car can have engine trouble during

a big race. A driver can be eliminated early. But a dedicated team keeps racing.

Don Garlits

There are many famous top fuel drivers. One is Don Garlits. His nickname is Big Daddy.

When Garlits was 14 years old, he was repairing cars. In high school, he began racing in his hometown of Tampa, Florida. Later on, Garlits quit his job as a bookkeeper to become a professional racer.

Garlits' dragster is called the Swamp Rat. He was the first driver to top 180 miles (288 kilometers) per hour. He broke the 200-mile (320-kilometer) per-hour barrier in 1964. He was the first person to put the engine behind the driver. He made the change after an explosion nearly took off his right foot.

Don Prudhomme

Don Prudhomme is another famous top fuel driver. His nickname is The Snake.

Today, there are many famous top fuel drivers who are women, including Shelly Anderson.

Prudhomme grew up in Southern California. He became a professional top fueler at the age of 21. Before Prudhomme became a professional, he practiced every Sunday at a local drag strip. He has won many championships.

The Jr. Drag Racing League encourages young people who want to race.

Shirley Muldowney

Shirley Muldowney is another famous top fuel driver. She was born in Mount Clemens, Michigan.

At first, many drivers thought that Muldowney could not compete because she was a woman. But Muldowney insisted she be

judged on her driving, not her gender. She went
on to break several of Don Garlits' records.

Jr. Drag Racing League

Boys and girls between age eight and 17 can
drag race, too. They can join the Jr. Drag
Racing League (JDRL). The league is part of
the NHRA.

Young racers drive dragsters that are about
half the size of real top fuelers. They have
engines like those used in lawn mowers.
Someday, somebody from the junior
association may become a star.

The NHRA encourages young people in
other ways, too. The association sponsors
races, scholarships, and career fairs. It
organizes school field trips to racetracks. The
NHRA does everything it can do to promote
the future of drag racing.

Glossary

acceleration—the rate at which something changes speeds
class—separate category for different styles of vehicles
deafening—an extremely loud noise
debris—bits and pieces of litter
disqualify—kick out of a race
handicap—when a disadvantage is put on a racer to make the race more competitive
header—a single pipe that brings two or more pipes together to carry exhaust from the engine
heat—preliminary rounds of a race
pit—area away from the racetrack where mechanics work on vehicles
preliminary trial—another name for heat
sanction—officially approve
traction—the ability of something to grip a surface

To Learn More

Connolly, Maureen. *Dragsters.* Mankato, Minn.: Capstone Press, 1992.

Olney, Ross R. *Modern Drag Racing Superstars.* New York: Dodd, Mead & Co., 1981.

Smith, Jay. *Drag Racing.* Minneapolis: Capstone Press, 1995.

Sosa, Maria. *Dragsters.* Mankato, Minn.: Crestwood House, 1987.

Stambler, Irwin. *Top Fuelers: Drag Racing Royalty.* New York: G.P. Putnam's Sons, 1978.

You can read more about drag racing in *Junior Drag Racer* magazine.

Useful Addresses

Canadian Automobile Sports Clubs
693 Petrolia Road
Downsview, ON M3J 2N6
Canada

Midwest Drag Racing Magazine
3802 Tuttle
Danville, IL 61832

National Hot Rod Association/Jr. Drag Racing League
P.O. Box 5555
Glendora, CA 91740-0950

Popular Hot Rodding Magazine
12100 Wilshire Blvd., Suite 250
Los Angeles, CA 90025

Internet Sites

Drag Racing & Hi Performance Illustrated
http://www.dragracer.com/

Inside Motor Sports
http://www.symweb.com/insidemotorsports/

NHRA Online
http://www.goracing.com/nhra/

Tri 'S' Racing
http://www.cyberhighway.net/~nicks/

Index